THE SPACE PLANNER

A HOME DECORATING + DESIGN WORKBOOK

by Meg Mateo Ilasco

CHRONICLE BOOKS

Text and illustrations © 2006 Meg Mateo Ilasco
www.mateoilasco.com

Library of Congress Cataloging-in-Publication Data available.

ISBN-10: 0-8118-5290-3 ISBN-13: 978-0-8118-5290-6

Design by Tessa Lee

Typeset in SF Old Republic and Trade Gothic

Manufactured in China

Chronicle Books endeavors to use environmentally responsible
paper in its gift and stationery products.

10 9 8 7 6 5 4

Chronicle Books LLC
680 Second Street
San Francisco, CA 94107

www.chroniclebooks.com

CONTENTS

INTRODUCTION

Your home is essentially an empty box with a set of walls, a floor, and a ceiling. But of course it's more than that; it's the place where you busily prepare meals for your family, where you roam privately in your skivvies, or where you serve up a pitcher of your favorite libation as you entertain friends. Your interior design strategy should be rooted in that personal reality. Rather than serving as a storage space for your possessions or a pristine museum, a home should exude security, comfort, and an authentic expression of its residents.

Ideally, your home should be an extension of your personality—an outlet that allows you to display your imagination. More often, though, your home becomes a reflection of your life's demands, out-grown tastes, or unapologetic budget. You may have turned a blind eye to the Archie Bunker-esque recliner and torchiere lamp in your family room, but others may not be as tolerant. So, before someone you know and trust blindsides you with a guerilla makeover crew and exhibits your decorat-ing woes on national television, take matters into your own hands. Otherwise you may find yourself at the mercy of a renegade designer spray-painting your favorite sofa hot pink or transforming your fireplace into a fire-breathing tiki god. With that ample motivation, you will need a planning guide to help you prepare for a decorating makeover or do-over of your current surroundings—or maybe a new start in a new pad. Enter *The Space Planner*, a workbook that aims to demystify design by offering a streamlined process for crafting a person-alized home. Organized according to function, each room is represented by a section that supplies guide-lines and ideas to get your creative compass spin-ning, along with a lifestyle questionnaire, a budget sheet, and a supply of grid sheets. (Not to mention vinyl stickers representing a few showrooms' worth of furniture pieces at the end of the workbook.) By carefully collecting ideas and constructing plans, you can avoid time delays and costly mistakes, and may find yourself emboldened to test out different interior styles, experiment with new furniture arrangements, or even add or remove walls.

To start the design process and stimulate your creativity, you will analyze your expectations and aspirations for each room using the lifestyle questionnaire. Next, the budget sheet will bring any proposals into financial focus by dictating what details you can afford, where you can splurge, and where you may need to be innovative. Decorating fun truly emerges during the furniture planning stage, as you move vinyl furniture pieces on a laminated grid to evaluate various arrangements. Though it won't burn as many calories as literally moving cumbersome furniture, it will save you time and energy better devoted to your decorating strategy. After you've arrived at a few viable floor plans, you can transfer them onto the included grid sheets. How nice it will be to select from a variety of working plans for your room! As an added bonus, the workbook has a convenient

pocket serving as a style repository to hold photo-graphs, magazine clippings, paint chips, and swatches.

The Space Planner gives you a clean slate, with all your furnishings and finishes virtually removed; likewise, you should also begin unencumbered by preconceptions about how a room should look. Seating does not necessarily have to be aligned in an L-shaped configuration; artwork need not be centered above the sofa; nor must a bed be flanked by a pair of matching end tables. The next section, "Defining Space," will introduce you to some basic design concepts that will challenge any of your pre-programmed design formulas. As you absorb these concepts, your own design sensibility will begin to form, unleashing your potential to bring real creativity into your home.

Once you complete the workbook, you will graduate with an unfettered understanding of your signature decorating style. Maybe you'll find that you readily subscribe to the creed of hedonism ("the more, the merrier"), minimalism ("less is more"), or frugalism ("more bang for your buck"). Better yet, maybe you'll diversify your style portfolio. Whatever the case, the pages will yield a cultivated identity of your home, so that each room contributes a piece of your voice. You'll be on your way to improving your home and your quality of life, complete with plans to carry it out. With that, transforming your vision into three-dimensional reality will be the easy part.

DEFINING SPACE

Designing your space can be a daunting task, but it is an important one—almost as essential as maintaining a healthy diet and exercising often. We have both a physical and an emotional response to efficiency, comfort, and beauty in our environment. The further we strive to personalize our homes, the more it will fulfill these attributes.

So how do you bring your personality and decorative style into your home? Unless you've taken interior design classes or were born into a family with a fruitful style heritage, you're left to your own (and maybe your friends') devices when it comes to decorating. Your instinct may be burdened by traditional notions of the ideal home, family customs from your childhood, or shopping experiences in furniture showrooms. If your natural inclination directs you to place furnishings around the perimeter of a room; to reduce all furniture arrangements to sterile, symmetrical compositions; or to purchase an entire roomful of furniture in a single trip to the department store, decorating is likely an unrewarding and confusing experience. While it is easy to subscribe to a furniture program de rigueur—whether Scandinavian (IKEA), iconic mid-century modern (Design Within Reach), or contemporary Americana (Pottery Barn)—and insert its tribe of stock characters in your room, such rigidity can rob your room of real creativity.

As preconceived rules often produce stagnant spaces (at the same time rendering you a frustrated designer), you will need to reprogram your design intuition to develop your own unique stamp on your space. So where do you begin? It's best to grasp some basic design concepts. With this knowledge, your design confidence will grow and your design eye will sharpen. You'll even make more informed decisions on furniture purchases. Although learning the theory behind any subject—whether design or accounting—can be quite technical, *The Space Planner* has made it more digestible by discussing concepts (such as scale, symmetry, balance, color, and lighting) as they relate to carving out a sense of place.

A home, like a person, should have a layered identity. Each room becomes a vignette that contributes layers to this identity. Knowing this, decorating becomes something more than just making a room pretty. Of course, it's okay to simply make something pretty, but it's even better when your surroundings capture a mood and communicate a message while retaining their practical purpose at the same time. Of the various qualities your rooms can adopt, we will cover five: *intimate, open, harmonious, versatile,* and *eclectic*. Like a person, your home and the rooms within it can have multiple personalities.

INTIMATE SPACE

DEFINING SPACE

An intimate room envelops you. It's womblike, cozy, and absolutely comfortable. A feeling of close quarters is best achieved by filling the space with large pieces of furniture. As the room is a space for enjoying private moments, seating in an intimate space should be configured to accommodate two types of privacy: shared and individual. To provoke a shared moment, group seating pieces close together to articulate a space for conversation. A U-shaped arrangement is desirable, as people are seated face-to-face, unlike an L-shaped configuration, which forces you to turn your body to look at someone. For solitary time, you can reserve a soft, overstuffed armchair removed from the focal point of the room.

A sense of intimacy is further enhanced by detail-rich surroundings abundant with accessories, bold patterns, and a variety of textures. Furnishings should include some comfort-inspired pieces like a furry throw rug as well as tactile features like textured walls. Contrary to most domestic guidebooks which look upon clutter as the ultimate sin of any space, clutter—when arranged sculpturally or organized skillfully—can be transformed into a thing of beauty. Functional clutter, or items you use frequently, like plates, cups, utensils, and creamer and sugar containers, can be displayed on kitchen or dining room shelves to heighten a feeling of intimate familiarity. By showcasing these ubiquitous necessities, you are providing

FLOORING

The floor takes up a large amount of visual space in a room, so choosing an appropriate flooring material and color are essential. There are three types of flooring to consider: soft (like carpeting), resilient (like cork or linoleum), or hard (like stone or tile). Whatever your selection, the color of the floor should always complement the room's overall color scheme. Furthermore, transitions in flooring should flow nicely from one space to another. Although traditional wisdom may instruct you to switch from hardwood to tile just because you've reached kitchen, consider continuing the wood floors into the kitchen. Here are other considerations when selecting flooring:

- Area rugs can help define one living space from another.

- Wall-to-wall flooring extends a space and enlarges a small room.

- Flooring can introduce a pattern, which is a nice contrast to a room that consists of mostly solid colors.

- Carpet is a good way to bring bold color and texture into a room. If you're looking for a low-maintenance carpet, stick to earth tones with fleck patterns since they tend to camouflage dirt and discolorations. On the color spectrum, remember that light colored carpets allow dirt to show, but dark colors expose lint and dust.

- Your floor color should not match and bleed into your wall color or else the side effect is a floating sensation. Depending on the mood of your space (like intimate or open), choosing a dark floor will absorb light, whereas a polished floor will reflect light back into the space.

visitors with information about you and the activities that transpire in the space. Note that functional clutter is not a license to be messy, so make sure the copious details shown are ones used on a regular basis or that serve a real decorative purpose.

The mood of a room is inextricably tied to its function. Bedrooms, libraries, and dens are good examples of intimate spaces, as they often necessitate privacy and quiet introspection. Rooms with fireplaces are also fitting, because fire often stirs up feelings of warmth and comfort. Other rooms of this type are north-facing rooms or those that receive little sunlight. (Remember that lighting, whether natural or artificial, is not always about maximizing. It's about getting the right amount to contribute to the dramatic sense of the space.) Intimate spaces should use dark, rich colors with a matte finish since they absorb light and make walls feel closer. Even a minimalist approach that demands an abundance of whites and grays can be rendered more intimate by introducing color through dark wood finishes and even plants.

OPEN SPACE

Having an open space does not necessarily mean having an open floor plan and minimal furnishings. (In fact, using a scant amount of furniture does not always make a space seem larger.) An open space exudes a sense of flowing and vibrant energy. To this end, you will want to bring in details that fit this airy vocabulary, such as light, pale-tone colors with a reflective finish to make walls recede, furnishings that aren't heavy on the eye (such as Lucite or white furniture instead of dark woods), and sheer window treatments that float about in a breeze. Lighting is another key ingredient in an open space, so you will want to bring in as much light as you can day or night. South-facing rooms or rooms that receive a lot of natural sunlight are obvious candidates for open spaces. Rooms that would benefit from a feeling of openness are areas for entertaining groups of people or accommodating many activities, such as kitchens, living rooms, and family rooms.

Openness is not a quality reserved only for large rooms. It can be achieved in any type of room, from the grandest living room to the smallest powder room. If you are wondering how you can have a sense of openness in a small room, the key is enhancing the perceived size though creative illusions. A particularly effective method is manipulating depth by using mirrors to open up the space. Another visual trick involves extending the views in a room so that the viewer sees more than just the room's immediate surroundings.

OUTDOOR

Thinking about plopping a standard patio set in your backyard? Think again. Bringing about a feeling of unity to your outdoor spaces and interior spaces will render your overall design more cohesive. The outdoors should become an extension of the interior and not a separate space. Blurring the boundaries between indoor and outdoor is forged by a smooth transition through shared furnishings, flooring, upholstery fabrics, wood finishes, surfaces, or accessories. The flow does not have to be from inside to outside, it can travel in the opposite direction as well through bringing outdoor organic textures inside. Recognize that gardens and outdoor spaces also become a part of the indoor when viewed from inside the home, so the placement of objects is crucial. It is particularly important to leave vistas open and free of large plants or furniture.

WINDOW TREATMENTS

Window treatments satisfy both functional and decorative pursuits. In addition to adding a layer of texture, color, or decorative interest to integrate the wall into your design scheme, they also shield for privacy, regulate the amount of light and glare, and can modify the perspective of an irregular window's shape or placement.

- **Protecting your privacy.** For all-day privacy, consider a combination of sheer and heavy drapery. Sheer draperies protect your privacy during the day while filtering light and giving the space a soft glow. Opaque draperies shield the nighttime view while adding texture and color to your room. Café curtains, which hang on the lower half of a window, are a good treatment for semi-privacy. From the inside, the lower half can block an unsightly street view while preserving a skyward view on the upper half. From the outside, they diminish the unobscured view into the home.

• Visual trickery.
To emphasize the verticality of a room as well as enhance the size of your windows, position curtain rods at the top of the wall (instead of immediately above the window frame) and allow the curtains to fall to the floor. If your windows are set disproportionately high on a wall, arranging low cabinets or shelving immediately below them will visually pull the windows down and create a more balanced view. If a window is width-starved, avoid treatments placed inside the frame and instead hang curtains on a rod wider than the window. Conversely, if you feel a window is too wide, stick to contained treatments like blinds or shutters.

• Retaining heat.
Heat loss happens through windows, so using drapes made of thick, heavy fabric (especially if gathered) will keep the room warmer. When neither privacy nor heat loss (i.e., with double-glazed windows) is an issue, consider theatrical window coverings that are more for display than function. For example, setting up long, flowing curtains that gracefully puddle on the floor elicits the same aesthetic as an exquisite train on a gown.

• Leave it bare.
Don't feel compelled to dress up all your windows. A bare window guarantees that decoration will not compete with its architectural integrity or the attractive view that it's framing.

For example, you can modify the position of a chair to create glimpses into other spaces, whether through a wall opening or a window. To really liberate a space, grab a sledgehammer to remove nonstructural walls, or install an additional or larger window to really bring the outdoors in. Bleeding areas together through matching surfaces is another method that heightens spatial flow by diminishing the shift from one room to another. For instance, if you have a combination kitchen-dining-family room, by using the same flooring and wall colors throughout, it will read as one large space instead of three smaller ones. When you allow connected spaces to participate in a common design dialogue, they will collectively convey a space that feels much larger than their individual square footage.

HARMONIOUS SPACE

When an Eastern philosophy such as harmony is invoked, stereotypical images of rock gardens, candles, and fountains may flood your mind. In home design, reaching harmony is not about achieving a traditional Asian look, but instead utilizing elements based in nature such as symmetry, balance, and repetition. When an entire space imparts itself as being one rather than a collection of disparate objects, it becomes harmonious.

Symmetry and balance, besides being qualities found in nature, are some of our most basic visual cues. Our eyes are sensitive to the feeling of balance and will naturally search for it in our visual field. Thus, an obvious type of room that lends itself to harmony is one that is symmetrical and well-proportioned. However, if you have a room in a less-than-perfect shape, you can modify it using visual trickery to make it appear more symmetrical. Because we can instantly sense when something is lopsided, you will need to adjust the perceived center, like building a wall of shelves to counterbalance irregularly placed windows. Whether your room is naturally symmetrical or is made that way by appropriation, finding the "center" of the room is essential in placing the focal point. The focal point can be anything from a fireplace to a piece of art. From that central item, the rest of your design decisions should serve to emphasize or redirect attention.

SCALE

Scale is a method of connecting objects to one another with regard to size and proportion, from the smallest of decorative accessories to the size of the entire room. It is one of the most important devices to add drama to your space. Using a selection of furnishings and accessories in a range of sizes can truly energize a space. When everything in a room is the same size, it makes for a bland and unimaginative space. Your room should largely be made up of medium scale objects balanced with meticulously selected large and small objects. Here are some key rules for manipulating scale:

- Both small and spacious rooms need large-scale objects. Diminutive rooms will appear bigger, as the height of a tall object accentuates the vertical lines of a room. Grand rooms will feel more intimate, as large objects fill its space.

- To truly appreciate scale as well as gain a sense of balance, juxtapose large items against smaller items. For example, you can have a large painting tempered by a row of tiny ceramic bowls below it.

- Think horizontally. The size of the floor tiles and the width of a low coffee table contribute to scale too.

- Apply the same amount of design rigor to everything: Look at scale as you lay out furnishings in the entire room, as well as when you organize accessories on a mantle.

- Well-informed design always considers the entire context. Whenever you introduce a furnishing, you should reference it against the room's other furnishings to create a hierarchy of scale.

Another element found in nature is repetition. It has the ability to create a sense of interconnectivity in a particular living space as well as throughout the house. By grouping items of similar shapes, sizes, lines, colors, or angles, you can produce a repetitive composition. For instance, you can line up a bevy of matching bowls along a table in a pattern that evokes rhythm. Because harmonious schemes tend to be gridlike, it may be more interesting to vary the positioning of items to make the grouping arrhythmic. However, one element you should not repeat is the finish of furniture. Nothing dulls a room like an entire roomful of matching birch furnishings. When you repeat objects, be sure to moderate the frequency with which you introduce them into a space.

Considering all the above elements, acknowledge that excessive symmetry, balance, or repetition can turn your harmonious room into plain boring. You can introduce a touch of asymmetrical balance, like hanging a lamp off-center but equalizing it with a vase on the table below. In addition, to counter a monotonous, repetitive pattern like graphic wallpaper, you can add surprising, curious, or even humorous elements—like a pair of oversize animal sculptures. By working with as well as against the grain of harmony, your room will be more visually appealing.

VERSATILE SPACE

Although rooms are given labels to distinguish their function, a room is not limited to its name-sake. Your "living room" might be an all-in-one dining-family room; or your spaces may adopt multiple purposes, such as a guest bedroom that is also your home office. In cases like that, the goal is to give the room a fluid look that does not draw attention to its disjointed purposes. A modern home often has to be versatile, and so it should adapt to your changing needs.

Storage is a key element in versatile environments. Not all facets of a versatile room's functions need to be on display; like a chameleon, a room should make its transformation only when necessary. Consider furniture that is easily concealed, transported, wheeled, or folded, like a butterfly director's chair, nested tables, or a coffee table on casters. Multipurpose furniture, like a sofa bed that accommodates overnight visitors or an armoire that holds office equipment, can be an asset. Triple-duty items are also desirable innovations, such as seating cubes that function as storage, seating, and coffee table; or low shelving with cushions providing storage, seating, and even a spare bed. Versatile rooms may have to tolerate abuse from small children and general repetitive use, so you may want to invest in furniture fabrics that are durable and easy to care for, like canvas, linen, denim, sturdy cotton, or ultrasuede.

COLOR

Color can be a complex subject to tackle, but here are some simple, basic rules to follow:

- Dark walls and a light floor create a floating sensation.

- Light walls and a dark floor draw attention upward.

- Light colors make walls recede and emphasize a room's height.

- Dark colors stimulate a cozy feeling.

- Contrasting colors can divide a space. Monochromatic schemes emphasize spaciousness.

- Plants can also be a medium for introducing color.

- The perception of color is influenced by light. To avoid costly color mistakes, buy a quart of paint first. Paint test blocks in the room to see how the color is affected by both natural and artificial light.

LIGHTING

In recent years, lighting has taken center stage in interior design, as it is an essential component in establishing the drama of a room. It can direct a viewer's eye to different parts of a room for effect, such as highlighting pieces of artwork or directing attention away from awkward spaces. The four main types of lighting are natural, task, ambient, and decorative. *Natural lighting* is of course daylight. Keep in mind that it moves and changes in color and intensity throughout the day. *Task lighting* is strictly functional—at the desk in your home office, for instance; *ambient lighting* can radiate a softness or hue to evoke a special mood during, say, a celebratory dinner; and *decorative lighting* draws in the attention of visitors with innovative fixtures and eye-catching components.

- Use lighting theatrically to cast interesting shadows on the wall or create silhouettes of objects. Your lighting composition can become equal parts ambience and art installation.

- A decorative light, like a glamorous chandelier, is an excellent focal point for any room.

- Make sure you place lights at the correct height to achieve the proper effect.

- Be sure there is ample direct artificial lighting to help you accomplish a particular task, whether it's preparing food or reading.

- Bringing in an abundance of natural light will help a space feel open and vibrant. If a room receives too little natural light, remember that you can borrow light from other spaces by cutting openings in dividing walls.

- Because lighting plans usually come at the end of a renovation, its budget often ends up getting cut or reduced. When this is the case, maximize the amount of natural light you can bring in and use less expensive lighting to cover task and ambient needs.

Versatility also extends to the mood of a room—as it ultimately changes with function or even with the time of day. For example, a dining room that doubles as a home office will alternate between two distinctly different identities. That particular room will need attention when it comes to lighting, as it should conveniently switch modes to offer ample task lighting for working and atmospheric soft lighting for dining. Like night and day, a versatile room should have the capacity to transform from an energetic to a tranquil personality with relative ease.

ECLECTIC SPACE

Of the different personalities presented here, an eclectic room is the most extroverted, providing a never-ending source of fascination for anyone who visits it. It speaks the most about a resident's idiosyncrasies and creative voice, revealing the varied possessions they prize and their innovation to arrange them in a single space. But don't confuse being eclectic with being mismatched, disorganized, or random; an eclectic style may wed various styles, eras, themes, colors, shapes, or lines, but it does so in a seamless way.

Mastering a space such as this, you will become equal parts design curator and fearless alchemist. When displaying a collection of goods, the key is not to convert your room into a dizzying museum of stuff but to find a way to live in your art. Visitors should not be afraid to interact with and touch the items in the space. As a starting point, you should select a focal point to set the tone of the room. It's the first thing that draws a person in and introduces them to your dramatic space. More than likely, your focal point will be something from your collection, such as an eye-catching wall hanging or a one-off chair.

An eclectic room may be complex and full of character, but its complexity is always planned with deliberate intent. The composition of items is never arbitrary. To execute this skillfully, your design should incorporate elements of both unity and variety. As the human eye naturally

PASSAGEWAYS

Sadly, passageways are often neglected as merely avenues from one space into another. However, these transition spaces can be used to develop the mood by foreshadowing what's to come. Here are thoughts to bear in mind when working with passageways:

- Hallways can provide excellent perspectives into other spaces or frame a focal point at the end.

- Mirrors can effectively widen a narrow hallway.

- Consider durable and resilient flooring for frequently used passageways.

- Stairways should be decorated in a way that alludes to the room scheme to which it leads.

- If your staircase is a focal point, be sure that the background serves to enforce the architecture of the staircase, rather than take away from it. For example, if you want to highlight a sweeping, curving balustrade, you should position wall-hangings that follow this curve, or if you have a strong linear staircase, your wallpaper pattern should exhibit similar lines.

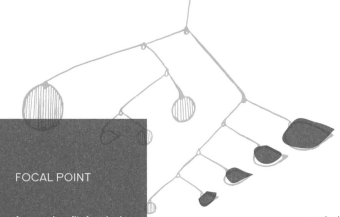

FOCAL POINT

Any room benefits from having a main attraction that draws a person into the space to investigate further. A focal point anchors the room and sets the mood. It could be the wall color, a composition of framed images, a fireplace, a one-off piece of furniture, a quirky piece of art, or a luxurious light fixture—whatever it may be, it demands the attention of the viewer. It's smart to let a focal point inform the rest of a room's design—or, if you've already designed a room and realize that it demands a major item to liven it up, you can introduce a piece that adds some zing.

wants to group similar objects together, your strategy will rely on repetition, be it the type of object, the color, or the shape. For instance, consider that a wall of vintage mirrors makes a stronger visual statement than does a distribution of individual mirrors throughout the space. Understandably, an eclectic style lends itself to an inclination for sensory overload. Be sure to have some white spaces, or areas devoid of visual activity, to allow the eye to rest.

If you're new to eclectic design, it may take several rounds of practice to conceive a look that is both comfortable and expressive of your voice. If you're a real design neophyte without a collection of treasures on hand, be patient and collect items slowly and carefully. Remember that a true eclectic style does not happen at once but is lovingly cultivated over time. Be selective about your acquisitions so that each has a purpose or story to share. If you succumb to the temptation to snatch up every piece of catnip dangling in front of you, you'll just be laden with a bunch of tchotchkes. In time, you may find yourself to be an intrepid master mixologist—juxtaposing old and new styles, repurposing utilitarian goods, turning mundane items into small masterpieces, cherishing imperfection, and frequently visiting antique shops and garage sales in search of one-of-a-kind treasures.

HOW TO
USE THE PLANNER

By now it should be clear that decorating is not all about aesthetics. It's about making a well-conceived space that recognizes a dual goal for your home: functionality and visual appeal. Because informed and intelligent design is specific to its users and its location, *The Space Planner* is organized by room function and equips each room's section with a set of guidelines and ideas, and the following helpful tools: a lifestyle questionnaire, a budget sheet, and grid worksheets.

LIFESTYLE QUESTIONNAIRE

This list of considerations will explore the room's current functions as well as your habits, expectations, and aspirations for the space. To give everyone a fair shake in the design process, your design should be inclusive of all voices, not just the ones in your head. So if you share your home with others, their input in the survey is equally essential. In forming the building blocks for your room design, you will ask yourself a battery of questions like:

What mood do I want for this room?
What colors would help me achieve that mood?
How can I design this room to achieve this mood?

By putting your thoughts and ideas on paper, you will lay the groundwork for your design solution. When it comes time to select materials, colors, finishes, furniture, and decor, you will be better prepared. It is this type of careful scrutiny that leads the way to the best design solutions and aesthetic decisions.

BUDGET SHEET

At face value, the cost of redecorating a 150-square-foot room may not sound like much, but multiply that by the number of rooms you have, and throw in finishes and furnishings, and the eventual sticker shock will hit you. A short-term and long-term budget sheet is included with each room to help you calculate where to skimp and maybe even splurge—and by how much, which is particularly helpful if you possess the unfortunate combination of a discerning taste coupled with shallow pockets. Although a design budget is the voice of reason, it is also one that can inspire much innovation.

As important as a beautiful environment is to your well-being, it does not justify going into major debt. Unless you can truly afford to drop big bucks on your projects, please don't start from scratch and buy everything new. Try instead to garner new appreciation for your possessions by teaching old objects new tricks. For example, books can have an occupation outside of reading material; when stacked, they can become a makeshift side table or a piece of sculpture. Buy only the furnishings necessary to accomplish your design, and make use of the furnishings you already own. Spending more will not necessarily render a room more beautiful, nor does spending less mean having a less alluring room.

FURNITURE PLANNING

Because furniture planning is the most interactive portion of this workbook, it may be tempting to skip ahead and start rearranging to your heart's desire. That can be fun, but devoid of context you will be merely shuffling forms around. Successful design is an informed process that always refers back to the problem, verifying that it is indeed reaching an appropriate solution. The questionnaire and budget sheet should be used as constant points of reference, validating that your floor plan is adequately working within the functions, desires, and budget of that space.

Generating a furniture plan for your room means first mapping out a floor plan. A good furniture strategy starts with an accurately measured room. Start by taking measurements of the room's perimeter and drawing a rough sketch of the room on the grid sheets. Include windows, doors, door openings, radiators, and stationary units (like built-in shelving and closets). Mark electrical plugs, phone jacks, and television outlets. Once you've sketched it, redraw it accurately on one of the laminated grids (located at the front and back of the book) using a dry-erase marker. The laminated grids, as well as the grid sheets in each chapter, are drawn at ¼" scale—that is, every square on the grid represents 1 foot of floor space. Once you've drawn the outline, double-check your work by recounting the squares.

Spaces don't operate independently of each other; so draw in parts of other spaces such as hallways, connecting rooms, and outdoor balconies too. Doing so will allow you to think about the visual perspectives from one space into another. Your design decisions in one room should inform all subsequent rooms. Especially with outdoor spaces, you want a sense of unity from the inside to the outside.

The vinyl furniture pieces in the back of the book are also at ¼" scale. The laminated grids will allow you to rearrange these vinyl stickers repeatedly. Measure your furniture to find which stickers most closely match your pieces. In the event that you don't find a corresponding sticker for an oddly shaped or unique piece you want to include, feel free to substitute something similar in size or to draw the piece in yourself with a dry-erase marker. When considering new furniture for your space, don't feel limited by the pieces that traditionally belong to a room category. Think about living room pieces for your bedroom, or dining room pieces for your kitchen. Also be open to the possibility of incorporating pieces of furniture you don't yet own or have never thought to purchase. Perhaps you want to know how a classic mid-century chaise lounge would look in your living room. There is a furniture sticker for that as well as many other desirable furniture pieces that aren't customary in most planning workbooks. You'll have a broad selection of furniture at your fingertips before you've invested a single dollar. Maybe it will even inspire you to save up for a few particularly appealing pieces.

Ideally, furniture placement is driven by function and comfort, aims to maximize versatility, and uses your visual instinct to create imaginative arrangements. As you move the pieces around, contemplate both positive and negative space. Positive space is defined by the actual furniture, whereas negative space is the "leftover" space. In regard to positive space, try to vary the geometry of the furniture pieces. When you have an array of furniture with too many right-angled corners, introduce a piece with rounded edges. The same strategy of variation applies to the negative space, or the spaces between objects; if furniture is arranged in too linear a fashion, try a circular formation to break it up.

Another visual concept to consider is zoning for different atmospheres within one room. Like a split personality, dual qualities such as intimate and open can exist in the same space. One way to differentiate between these qualities is to break up the room into a series of smaller spaces; some of the simplest and most cost-efficient methods to differentiate between zones are to introduce a rug, a screen, or even a block of wall color or ambient lighting to highlight a particular area. Another way is to use negative space with an eye toward the circulation patterns it creates. Diverting traffic away from an area zoned for

intimacy (like a niche for reading) and directing it closer to an area zoned for openness will preserve each area's unique character.

Even though you will be planning in two dimensions, you should always try to envision the space in 3-D, especially in regard to the scale of the furniture. Imagine what it would be like to stand or sit in different areas of the space. This is important in finding the perfect location for the room's focal point. When you've reached a viable floor plan, transfer it onto the included grid sheets. There you can use your plan to create a lighting strategy as well. Using colored pencils, first draw a set of lines showing where natural light comes in, and then another set of lines in a different color to indicate where more light is desirable. Strive for a sense of balance as you generate your lighting plan, so that you are not bestowing lighting priority to one part of the room while neglecting another.

As you can see, fabricating a floor plan is more than just shuffling furniture pieces around. In addition to arranging furniture, other important considerations are scale, zoning, and lighting. You should create several floor plan options to arrive at the optimal composition. As design is an interactive process, you should continually edit, refine, and improve your proposed layout. With these tools at your fingertips, you can be on your way to becoming a well-informed designer. Ready to start planning?

SPACE TO . . .

THE LIVING ROOM

SPACE TO ENTERTAIN

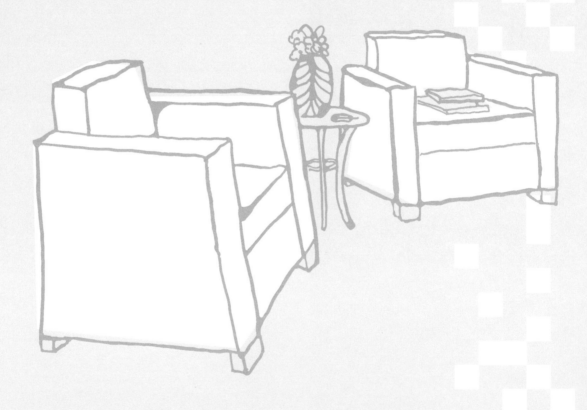

If ever there were a room suffering from an identity crisis, it's the living room. Contrary to its name, it has traditionally been the most decorated but least used space in a home. In stark contrast to the family room, which has the honor of providing the backdrop for daily activities, the living room gets occasional visits for dusting but otherwise sits like a bejeweled princess with no invitation to the ball. In your new decorating strategy, extend a friendly hand to the living room and allow it to join the party.

The living room should be sophisticated for entertaining, yet approachable to invite conversation, relaxation, or even play. This may mean breaking up the room into different types of zones to accommodate both private moments and group activities. Using the basic furniture components of a living room such as chairs, a sofa, a coffee table, and an area rug, you can construct simple zones. Area rugs clearly delineate one area from another. Furthermore, by simply positioning two armchairs to face each other, you've already set a stage for one-on-one conversation. Having a large sectional sofa wrapped around a substantial coffee table affords a space for playing games with a group. Remember that there should be

enough seating for all the inhabitants, to allow them to share the room in the same way at the same time. If you have one room that performs double duty as living and family room, zoning is helpful in creating formal and informal faces for the room. One area of the room can evoke the elegant tone of a formal living room, displaying your finest treasures, counterbalanced with a more casual area that invites day-to-day activities (see "Space to Relax [the Family Room]," page 34).

Breathing life into your living room is important, as it is the public face of your home and often the first room everyone sees. It sets the tone for the remainder of your home. As space is a sensory experience, the living room is a good place to display many of your possessions that are close to your heart so that visitors are compelled to walk around and investigate more closely. Through your design, your visitors will learn about you and the things you cherish in life.

LIFESTYLE QUESTIONNAIRE

What are the primary uses of or the most routine activities in this room?

. . . .

. . . .

. . . .

. . . .

. . . .

What other activities would I like to do in this room?

. . . .

. . . .

. . . .

. . . .

. . . .

What type of environment motivates me to do these activities?

. . . .

. . . .

. . . .

. . . .

. . . .

What do I like most about the room?

. . . .

. . . .

. . . .

What do I like least about the room?

. . . .

. . . .

. . . .

What are my design priorities for this room?

．．．

．．．

．．．

．．．

．．．

When does the room receive light?

．．．

．．．

．．．

What mood do I want for this room?

．．．

．．．

．．．

What colors would help me achieve that mood?

．．．

．．．

．．．

What furniture style do I want for this room?

．．．

．．．

．．．

How else can I design this room to achieve the desired mood?

．．．

．．．

．．．

BUDGET SHEET

FINISHES		SHORT TERM	LONG TERM
	Wall preparation	$	$
	Paint	$	$
	Wallpaper	$	$
	Trim	$	$
FLOORING			
	Carpet	$	$
	Rugs	$	$
	Hardwood	$	$
	Tile/Stone	$	$
	Vinyl/Other	$	$
FURNISHINGS			
	Fireplace	$	$
	Sofas	$	$
	Chairs	$	$
	Benches/Ottomans	$	$
	Side tables	$	$
	Coffee table	$	$
	Armoire	$	$
	Credenzas	$	$
	Shelves/Storage	$	$
	Mirrors	$	$
	Built-ins	$	$

		SHORT TERM	LONG TERM
WINDOW TREATMENTS			
	Hardware	$ _____	$ _____
	Curtains	$ _____	$ _____
	Shades/Blinds	$ _____	$ _____
LIGHTING			
	Wall sconces	$ _____	$ _____
	Picture lights	$ _____	$ _____
	Pendant fixtures	$ _____	$ _____
	Floor lamps	$ _____	$ _____
	Table lamps	$ _____	$ _____
ACCESSORIES			
	Television	$ _____	$ _____
	Video/DVD/Stereo	$ _____	$ _____
	Pillows/Cushions	$ _____	$ _____
	Pictures/Paintings	$ _____	$ _____
	Vases/Ceramics	$ _____	$ _____
	Antiques	$ _____	$ _____
	Plants	$ _____	$ _____
OTHER:			
_____		$ _____	$ _____
_____		$ _____	$ _____
_____		$ _____	$ _____
_____		$ _____	$ _____
_____		$ _____	$ _____
	TOTAL	$ _____	$ _____

29

WORKSHEET I

THE LIVING ROOM

$^1\!/_4$" = 1'

WORKSHEET 2

THE LIVING ROOM

¼" = 1'

THE FAMILY ROOM

SPACE TO RELAX

If the living room is the public face of your home and your bedroom is the private face, the family room hangs somewhere in the balance. As opposed to the more sophisticated tone of the living room (see "Space to Entertain—the Living Room," page 24), a family room, as the name implies, is the staging ground for everyday life. It can be an extremely social space filled with chaotic traffic, noisy banter, and group activities. It is the space where you should feel the most at home.

In this room, seating is the first order of business. The sectional sofa is a family room favorite, as it is large enough to accommodate seating and even resting for several people at a time. Best of all, it can even double as a place for overnight guests to sleep. Because of repeated use, you should choose durable, easy-to-clean fabrics for your sofas and chairs. Facing the seating is the room's likely main activity, the television. As entertainment media has become increasingly sophisticated and intricate, many opt for a clean look that oftentimes displays the TV screen but hides the DVD player, the TiVo box, and the home theater components behind cabinet doors. You can choose to follow this approach, or if you're

stimuli-driven and prefer a room akin to the Starship Enterprise bridge with blinking lights and technology abounding, you can choose to showcase the many metal boxes of varying sizes and styles.

The "hide versus reveal" discussion extends to the other activities that transpire in a family room. The various accoutrements involved, such as reading materials, game boards, videogames, and kids' crafts, can often cause unwanted clutter. It can be stashed out of sight inside cabinetry or, ideally, can be incorporated into the room through open shelving to reflect the room's functions. For instance, if you use the room for your hobbies, you can incorporate a craft table or a sewing machine ensemble into the design of the room. When these personal, everyday activities and their accessories are displayed, it increases the feeling of intimacy and gives an obvious nod to the reality of the space.

LIFESTYLE QUESTIONNAIRE

What are the primary uses of or the most routine activities in this room?

. . . .

. . . .

. . . .

. . . .

. . . .

What other activities would I like to do in this room?

. . . .

. . . .

. . . .

. . . .

. . . .

What type of environment motivates me to do these activities?

. . . .

. . . .

. . . .

. . . .

. . . .

What do I like most about the room?

. . . .

. . . .

. . . .

What do I like least about the room?

. . . .

. . . .

. . . .

What are my design priorities for this room?

....

....

....

....

....

When does the room receive light?

....

....

....

What mood do I want for this room?

....

....

....

What colors would help me achieve that mood?

....

....

....

What furniture style do I want for this room?

....

....

....

How else can I design this room to achieve the desired mood?

....

....

....

BUDGET SHEET

THE FAMILY ROOM

38

		SHORT TERM	LONG TERM
FINISHES			
	Wall preparation	$	$
	Paint	$	$
	Wallpaper	$	$
	Trim	$	$
FLOORING			
	Carpet	$	$
	Rugs	$	$
	Hardwood	$	$
	Tile/Stone	$	$
	Vinyl/Other	$	$
FURNISHINGS			
	Fireplace	$	$
	Sofas	$	$
	Chairs	$	$
	Benches/Ottomans	$	$
	Side tables	$	$
	Coffee table	$	$
	Armoire	$	$
	Credenzas	$	$
	Shelves/Storage	$	$
	Mirrors	$	$
	Built-ins	$	$

		SHORT TERM	LONG TERM
WINDOW TREATMENTS			
	Hardware	$	$
	Curtains	$	$
	Shades/Blinds	$	$
LIGHTING			
	Wall sconces	$	$
	Picture lights	$	$
	Pendant fixtures	$	$
	Floor lamps	$	$
	Table lamps	$	$
ACCESSORIES			
	Television	$	$
	Video/DVD/Stereo	$	$
	Pillows/Cushions	$	$
	Pictures/Paintings	$	$
	Vases/Ceramics	$	$
	Antiques	$	$
	Plants	$	$
OTHER:			
		$	$
		$	$
		$	$
		$	$
		$	$
	TOTAL	$	$

WORKSHEET 1

THE FAMILY ROOM

1/4" = 1'

WORKSHEET 2

THE FAMILY ROOM

¼" = 1'

THE KITCHEN

Designing a kitchen usually falls into two camps: Dressing it up as a pristine culinary showpiece or equipping it to be a functioning, active space that evokes real life. Maybe you want something in between: an attractive kitchen with just enough shades of reality. Whichever your preference, your kitchen should be designed with efficiency, function, convenience, and safety in mind. Turning a lackluster workhorse into a culinary masterpiece can be a very expensive endeavor indeed. Your budget will probably be the most important part of planning your kitchen, as you can easily spend thousands of dollars on appliances alone. Perhaps you can find a middle ground, such as simply coating your cabinetry with paint and updating its hardware, rather than replacing it altogether.

As you draw up plans for your kitchen, consider the primary purposes you'd use the space for, whether cooking, casual entertaining, hobbies, or office activity. If food preparation and cooking are the primary activities you envision, organize your space so that you can complete your tasks with a minimum amount of distraction. To improve workflow, the pathways between the refrigerator, sink, food preparation counter, and stove should not be cramped or obscured with traffic obstacles. Optimally, the refrigerator should be situated away from heat sources (like the stove) and close to the entrance so that people don't traverse the entire kitchen when making a beeline for a can of cold soda.

If you're the take-out type, organizing your space will not be as critical as creating a kitchen that wows your guests. Despite what others may tell you, don't be too quick to jump on the granite countertop and wall-to-wall stainless steel bandwagon without first considering the amazing array of material possibilities available to you. Consider industrial, ridged Lexan Thermoclear back-splashes, rustic terra-cotta tiles with a beautiful patina, or smooth, contemporary laminate countertops. With their varied textures, these materials can help enhance a space's sensory experience.

LIFESTYLE QUESTIONNAIRE

What are the primary uses of or the most routine activities in this room?

. . . .

. . . .

. . . .

. . . .

. . . .

What other activities would I like to do in this room?

. . . .

. . . .

. . . .

. . . .

. . . .

What type of environment motivates me to do these activities?

. . . .

. . . .

. . . .

. . . .

. . . .

What do I like most about the room?

. . . .

. . . .

. . . .

What do I like least about the room?

. . . .

. . . .

. . . .

What are my design priorities for this room?

When does the room receive light?

What mood do I want for this room?

What colors would help me achieve that mood?

What furniture style do I want for this room?

How else can I design this room to achieve the desired mood?

BUDGET SHEET

		SHORT TERM	LONG TERM
FINISHES			
	Wall preparation	$	$
	Paint	$	$
	Wallpaper	$	$
	Backsplash	$	$
	Trim	$	$
FLOORING			
	Carpet	$	$
	Rugs	$	$
	Hardwood	$	$
	Tile/Stone	$	$
	Vinyl/Other	$	$
APPLIANCES / FIXTURES / FURNISHINGS			
	Refrigerator	$	$
	Stove	$	$
	Sink	$	$
	Extractor hood	$	$
	Microwave	$	$
	Dishwasher	$	$
	Waste disposal	$	$
	Countertops	$	$
	Cabinets	$	$
	Tables	$	$
	Stools/Chairs	$	$
	Benches	$	$
	Shelves/Storage	$	$

		SHORT TERM	LONG TERM
WINDOW TREATMENTS			
	Hardware	$	$
	Curtains	$	$
	Shades/Blinds	$	$
LIGHTING			
	Wall sconces	$	$
	Picture lights	$	$
	Chandelier	$	$
	Pendant fixtures	$	$
	Floor lamps	$	$
	Table lamps	$	$
ACCESSORIES			
	Pots/Pans	$	$
	Pictures/Paintings	$	$
	Vases/Ceramics	$	$
	Antiques	$	$
	Plants	$	$
OTHER:			
		$	$
		$	$
		$	$
		$	$
		$	$
		$	$
	TOTAL	$	$

WORKSHEET I

THE KITCHEN

1/4" = 1'

WORKSHEET 2

THE KITCHEN

1/4" = 1'

THE DINING ROOM

The dining room is a privileged chamber, bearing witness to a variety of occasions and milestones, from everyday meals and dinner parties to birthday celebrations and holiday gatherings. In some homes, the dining room sees infrequent use, especially when a breakfast nook accommodates daily meals. For the space-starved among us, this room then becomes a perfect candidate to assume other identities, such as a part-time home office. Whether you choose to use the room only for special events or for everyday functions, you can fill it with visual and dramatic allure.

The focus of any dining room is the dining table and chairs. You should choose a table that is in proportion to the total size of the room. If you have an expansive room, you don't want a diminutive table for four; instead, use a large banquet table with settings for eight or ten. It might be helpful to think beyond the traditional sense when arranging the table and chairs. The chairs do not necessarily have to be placed in an orderly, equidistant fashion about the table. For effect, you can arrange them in an arrhythmic pattern, with some chairs bunched close together and others strewn farther apart. You can even experiment by mixing chair styles or using a bench in combination with chairs.

Because events like dinner parties usually occur in the evening, proper lighting becomes a key issue. Dining lighting is typically soft, to establish the atmosphere and mood. Whether you're striving for a fabulous get-together or a quiet evening à deux, the right mood can enhance any meal, conversation, or interaction. If you use the dining room every day, good lighting can make an otherwise ordinary meal feel like a dinner in a fine restaurant.

LIFESTYLE QUESTIONNAIRE

What are the primary uses of or the most routine activities in this room?

. . . .

What other activities would I like to do in this room?

. . . .

What type of environment motivates me to do these activities?

. . . .

What do I like most about the room?

. . . .

What do I like least about the room?

. . . .

What are my design priorities for this room?

When does the room receive light?

What mood do I want for this room?

What colors would help me achieve that mood?

What furniture style do I want for this room?

How else can I design this room to achieve the desired mood?

BUDGET SHEET

		SHORT TERM	LONG TERM
FINISHES			
	Wall preparation	$	$
	Paint	$	$
	Wallpaper	$	$
	Trim	$	$
FLOORING			
	Carpet	$	$
	Rugs	$	$
	Hardwood	$	$
	Tile/Stone	$	$
	Vinyl/Other	$	$
FURNISHINGS			
	Dining table	$	$
	Chairs/Benches	$	$
	Side tables	$	$
	Credenzas	$	$
	Mirrors	$	$
	Shelves/Storage	$	$
	Built-ins	$	$

		SHORT TERM	LONG TERM
WINDOW TREATMENTS			
	Hardware	$	$
	Curtains	$	$
	Shades/Blinds	$	$
LIGHTING			
	Wall sconces	$	$
	Picture lights	$	$
	Chandelier	$	$
	Pendant fixtures	$	$
	Floor lamps	$	$
	Table lamps	$	$
ACCESSORIES			
	Table linens	$	$
	Dishes	$	$
	Flatware	$	$
	Pictures/Paintings	$	$
	Vases/Ceramics	$	$
	Antiques	$	$
	Plants	$	$
OTHER:			
		$	$
		$	$
		$	$
		$	$
	TOTAL	$	$

WORKSHEET 1

THE DINING ROOM

1/4" = 1'

WORKSHEET 2

THE DINING ROOM

$\frac{1}{4}" = 1'$

THE MASTER BEDROOM

The master bedroom is one of the most private areas in the house and therefore should be an expression of the real you. It's one of the few places in your home where you can truly be as extravagant, flamboyant, imaginative, or maybe even modest and introspective as you desire. To enhance your sensory experience, you should keep an eye toward objects that boost relaxation, reflection, or renewal. Understandably, it has to be a reliably quiet place—a sanctuary in which to escape from everyday life.

Because we spend one-third of our lives sleeping, our bed needs to be absolutely comfortable to nurture our bodies and lull us into restful sleep. The bed is usually the largest item in the space and should rightfully dominate it. Make sure other pieces, like a bulky armoire, don't compete for attention. Beyond sleeping, a range of activities can happen in the master bedroom— cuddling with your partner, exercising, watching television, getting dressed, doing work, playing with your children, or eating breakfast in bed. Indeed, a full day can be spent in this room— so make sure that there are appropriate furnishings as well as sufficient storage for the items that accompany your activities.

Even though we spend most of the time in our bedroom with our eyes closed, it doesn't mean the decor should make you snore. You can follow traditional wisdom and embrace colors that are soothing and tranquil. But color is a personal and subjective choice. This is your space, so you should feel free to design around bright colors like scarlet red or tangerine, if you wish. Just remember to have discretion when you apply bold colors. You want just enough punch without overwhelming or disturbing the peace.

LIFESTYLE QUESTIONNAIRE

What are the primary uses of or the most routine activities in this room?

....

....

....

....

....

What other activities would I like to do in this room?

....

....

....

....

....

What type of environment motivates me to do these activities?

....

....

....

....

....

What do I like most about the room?

....

....

....

What do I like least about the room?

....

....

....

What are my design priorities for this room?

· ·

· ·

· ·

· ·

· ·

When does the room receive light?

· ·

· ·

· ·

What mood do I want for this room?

· ·

· ·

· ·

What colors would help me achieve that mood?

· ·

· ·

· ·

What furniture style do I want for this room?

· ·

· ·

· ·

How else can I design this room to achieve the desired mood?

· ·

· ·

· ·

BUDGET SHEET

		SHORT TERM	LONG TERM
FINISHES			
	Wall preparation	$	$
	Paint	$	$
	Wallpaper	$	$
	Trim	$	$
FLOORING			
	Carpet	$	$
	Rugs	$	$
	Hardwood	$	$
	Tile/Stone	$	$
	Vinyl/Other	$	$
FURNISHINGS			
	Bed	$	$
	Chairs	$	$
	Benches/Ottomans	$	$
	Side tables	$	$
	Dressers	$	$
	Armoire	$	$
	Credenzas	$	$
	Mirrors	$	$
	Fireplace	$	$
	Shelves/Storage	$	$
	Built-ins	$	$

	SHORT TERM	LONG TERM
WINDOW TREATMENTS		
Hardware	$	$
Curtains	$	$
Shades/Blinds	$	$
LIGHTING		
Wall sconces	$	$
Picture lights	$	$
Pendant fixtures	$	$
Floor lamps	$	$
Table lamps	$	$
ACCESSORIES		
Television	$	$
Video/DVD/Stereo	$	$
Exercise equipment	$	$
Pillows/Cushions	$	$
Bed linens	$	$
Pictures/Paintings	$	$
Vases/Ceramics	$	$
Antiques	$	$
Plants	$	$
OTHER:		
	$	$
	$	$
	$	$
TOTAL	$	$

WORKSHEET I

THE MASTER BEDROOM

¹/₄" = 1'

WORKSHEET 2

THE MASTER BEDROOM

$^1/_4$" = 1'

THE BEDROOMS

Everyone in your home needs a tranquil retreat for sleeping and dreaming. As you seek to establish a personal stamp on your space, the primary resident of each respective room is equally as eager to experiment in their small space. Like you, they may be teeming with excitement to give their space a signature focus, whether it's robotic toys or a collection of classic movie posters. When it comes to small children, you should present a flexible style that is playful and colorful and accommodates their goods without relying on gimmicky television characters or a similar thematic scheme. Because children's tastes in entertainment evolve quickly, suggest whimsical and graphic patterns like prints, dots, squares, or stripes instead. You should find a style that grows with your child. If you have a teenager, allow him to express his individuality, but provide guidance in the design process. The room should remain within the scope of your home design but rest in a middle ground that preserves his privacy and expresses his creative needs.

If you have a guest bedroom to design, the room should be a reflection of your thoughtful hospitality. Demonstrating your attention to visitors' needs, it should offer many of the standard amenities found in hotels (minus the overpriced minibar and drab bed linens). To ensure an enjoyable night of sleep, provide a comfortable mattress, extra blankets, and pillows. Additionally, a comfortable chair and a bedside table with an alarm clock, lamp, and reading material are equally pleasing should your guests want to retreat to their room. For that extra touch of thoughtfulness, the reading material can even be tailored to their taste, whether it's the latest copy of *InStyle,* the *New Yorker,* or *Sunset.* This tailoring can extend to the aesthetic considerations of the room as well. Imagining your typical or frequent visitor, whether it's your in-laws, college friends, or guests from abroad, you can use one group as inspiration to dictate the overall style of the room. The best way to know if you've reached your hospitable objective is to give your guest room a test-spin and spend a night there. If you enjoy your stay in the room, it's likely they will too.

LIFESTYLE QUESTIONNAIRE

What are the primary uses of or the most routine activities in this room?

....

....

....

....

....

What other activities would I like to do in this room?

....

....

....

....

....

What type of environment motivates me to do these activities?

....

....

....

....

....

What do I like most about the room?

....

....

....

What do I like least about the room?

....

....

....

What are my design priorities for this room?

....

....

....

....

....

When does the room receive light?

....

....

....

What mood do I want for this room?

....

....

....

What colors would help me achieve that mood?

....

....

....

What furniture style do I want for this room?

....

....

....

How else can I design this room to achieve the desired mood?

....

....

....

BUDGET SHEET

	SHORT TERM	LONG TERM
FINISHES		
Wall preparation	$	$
Paint	$	$
Wallpaper	$	$
Trim	$	$
FLOORING		
Carpet	$	$
Rugs	$	$
Hardwood	$	$
Tile/Stone	$	$
Vinyl/Other	$	$
FURNISHINGS		
Bed(s)	$	$
Chairs	$	$
Benches/Ottomans	$	$
Side tables	$	$
Dressers	$	$
Armoire	$	$
Credenzas	$	$
Mirrors	$	$
Shelves/Storage	$	$
Built-ins	$	$

	SHORT TERM	LONG TERM
WINDOW TREATMENTS		
Hardware	$	$
Curtains	$	$
Shades/Blinds	$	$
LIGHTING		
Wall sconces	$	$
Picture lights	$	$
Pendant fixtures	$	$
Floor lamps	$	$
Table lamps	$	$
ACCESSORIES		
Television	$	$
Video/DVD/Stereo	$	$
Exercise equipment	$	$
Pillows/Cushions	$	$
Bed linens	$	$
Pictures/Paintings	$	$
Vases/Ceramics	$	$
Antiques	$	$
Plants	$	$
OTHER:		
	$	$
	$	$
	$	$
TOTAL	$	$

WORKSHEET I

THE BEDROOMS

$^1/_4"$ = 1'

WORKSHEET 2

THE BEDROOMS

$^1/_4" = 1'$

WORKSHEET 3

THE BEDROOMS

THE OFFICE/DEN/LIBRARY

Your office can be a strictly utilitarian space, but it doesn't need to subscribe to office decor conventions. The last thing you want is for your home office to look like something from a cubicle farm. The home office should fit into the overall style of your home but not stand out. It should be a space that motivates you to work and stimulates your creativity. It should also include personal effects that humanize your workspace, such as plants, photographs, and art.

Take into consideration how often you plan on using this space and whether you'll use it for occasional office tasks or full-time work. If you're in the process of selecting a room to transform into an office, it's a good idea to pick one away from the hubbub of high-traffic areas, especially if you need to work in privacy and without constant interruptions. An underutilized room like the dining room is a great candidate for a home office. If you will use your office to meet with clients or colleagues, consider issues of access and meeting space. You will want a room that can be accessed without having to travel through the more private areas of the house—in some cases, that may mean turning your garage into an office.

Every workspace should be efficient and provide the least amount of distractions. Items used frequently, like the printer, the telephone, and the electrical outlets, should be conveniently located. In addition, you should give yourself sufficient surface space for non-computer activities. If an extra-clean work environment suits you best, leave your desk free of clutter with just the necessary items you use on a daily basis. However, if a large array of visual stimuli is the most desirable creative atmosphere, not every surface needs to be cleared. For you, functional clutter such as color swatches, magazine tear sheets, or even supplies like cans of ink and paint can be turned into a smart wall collage.

Any modern office has a barrage of cables, but you should keep them out of sight for both aesthetic and safety concerns. Storage is equally vital, so calculate how much space you need to dedicate to bookcases and shelving units. If you're considering wall-to-wall shelving, built-in ceiling-height wall units maximize storage and display options while giving the room a solid appearance.

Without a doubt, the workstation is the heart of a home office. Because you will spend many hours there engrossed in a particular activity, it should be as comfortable and ergonomic as possible. Regardless of how beautiful a chair is or how well it works in your design scheme, if it is not adjustable or set to the correct height (so that your forearm is parallel to the table), you will not enjoy working there. As natural light stimulates work, you should position the workstation so that light is maximized without glare. For times when natural light is unavailable, provide yourself with ample task lighting to prevent any eyestrain. The bottom line remains: When it comes to your working environment, comfort should always reign over aesthetics.

LIFESTYLE QUESTIONNAIRE

What are the primary uses of or the most routine activities in this room?

. . . .

What other activities would I like to do in this room?

. . . .

What type of environment motivates me to do these activities?

. . . .

What do I like most about the room?

. . . .

What do I like least about the room?

. . . .

What are my design priorities for this room?

....
....
....
....
....

When does the room receive light?

....
....
....

What mood do I want for this room?

....
....
....

What colors would help me achieve that mood?

....
....
....

What furniture style do I want for this room?

....
....
....

How else can I design this room to achieve the desired mood?

....
....
....

BUDGET SHEET

	SHORT TERM	LONG TERM
FINISHES		
Wall preparation	$	$
Paint	$	$
Wallpaper	$	$
Trim	$	$
FLOORING		
Carpet	$	$
Rugs	$	$
Hardwood	$	$
Tile/Stone	$	$
Vinyl/Other	$	$
FURNISHINGS		
Workstation	$	$
Desk	$	$
Tables	$	$
Sofas	$	$
Chairs	$	$
Benches/Ottomans	$	$
Side tables	$	$
Armoire	$	$
Credenzas	$	$
Shelves/Storage	$	$
Mirrors	$	$
Built-ins	$	$

	SHORT TERM	LONG TERM

WINDOW TREATMENTS

	SHORT TERM	LONG TERM
Hardware	$	$
Curtains	$	$
Shades/Blinds	$	$

LIGHTING

	SHORT TERM	LONG TERM
Wall sconces	$	$
Picture lights	$	$
Pendant fixtures	$	$
Floor lamps	$	$
Table lamps	$	$

ACCESSORIES

	SHORT TERM	LONG TERM
Computer	$	$
Containers	$	$
Pillows/Cushions	$	$
Pictures/Paintings	$	$
Vases/Ceramics	$	$
Antiques	$	$
Plants	$	$

OTHER:

	SHORT TERM	LONG TERM
	$	$
	$	$
	$	$
	$	$
	$	$

| **TOTAL** | $ | $ |

WORKSHEET I

THE OFFICE/DEN/LIBRARY

¹/₄" = 1'

WORKSHEET 2

$^1/_4" = 1'$

THE MASTER BATH

Gone are the days when master bathrooms were merely utilitarian spaces. Over the past few decades, the master bathroom has evolved into a status symbol, becoming a focal point for many homes. Residents take pride in showcasing their private getaway for calm and luxury, often incorporating elegant materials and sculptural fixtures. Daily rituals are anything but routine. Showers and tubs have become the conduit for mini-spa experiences, whether a few private minutes are spent getting a full-body massage from multiple showerheads or soaking in warm, aromatic bubbles. Nowadays, master bathrooms often open up into the main bedroom and offer extra space for activities beyond the usual hygienic functions, such as dressing or exercising. To provide for an experience closer to nature, some unique bathrooms connect to a backyard garden or even bring the outdoors in by incorporating a garden into the tub design scheme.

As visually alluring as your master bathroom should be, it should not override the importance of function and efficiency. The fixtures, no matter how much they may resemble the elegant necks of swans, must operate and function with ease. Surfaces must be pleasant to the touch and be able to withstand water and steam. Ergonomic concerns are especially important with items that are used routinely, so pay particular attention to the height of a sink or tub. You don't want to be hunched over a sink or have difficulty getting into or out of your tub. That will turn your tranquil dreams into chronic neck or back pain.

A perfect union of performance and style should also be apparent in all the usual components: a tub, a shower, dual vanities and washbasins, a toilet, and storage space. It's common to organize the bathroom around the bathtub, as many are very sculptural in shape; a sumptuous clawfoot or whirlpool tub is often the epitome of indulgence. A shower can be scaled down to its bare-bones functionality—or, if your imagination dictates otherwise, luxuriously tiled or integrated with your tub. Remember too that a bathroom requires much storage for toiletries and towels, and so you will need to figure out how much of it will be on display or hidden from view.

Bathrooms guided by the triple mantra of peace, quiet, and renewal should introduce comfortable pieces of furniture to soften the room, as it is normally full of hard surfaces. Cool, light colors are best to open up the space and instill a feeling of tranquility. To use lighting to continue this effect, bring in as much daylight as you can with strategically placed windows, or brighten the room with pink- or warm-toned artificial lights for a more soothing effect. For extra ambience, nothing underscores relaxation like candlelight.

And of course, many houses and apartments get by just fine with a single bathroom, in which the elegance of a master bathroom overlaps with the utilitarian needs of the everyday (see "Space to Bathe—the Bathrooms," page 106).

LIFESTYLE QUESTIONNAIRE

What are the primary uses of or the most routine activities in this room?

. . . .

. . . .

. . . .

. . . .

. . . .

What other activities would I like to do in this room?

. . . .

. . . .

. . . .

. . . .

. . . .

What type of environment motivates me to do these activities?

. . . .

. . . .

. . . .

. . . .

. . . .

What do I like most about the room?

. . . .

. . . .

. . . .

What do I like least about the room?

. . . .

. . . .

. . . .

What are my design priorities for this room?

. . . .

When does the room receive light?

. . . .

What mood do I want for this room?

. . . .

What colors would help me achieve that mood?

. . . .

What furniture style do I want for this room?

. . . .

How else can I design this room to achieve the desired mood?

. . . .

BUDGET SHEET

	SHORT TERM	LONG TERM
FINISHES		
Wall preparation	$	$
Paint	$	$
Wallpaper	$	$
Tile walls	$	$
Trim	$	$
FLOORING		
Carpet	$	$
Rugs	$	$
Hardwood	$	$
Tile/Stone	$	$
Vinyl/Other	$	$
FIXTURES / FURNISHINGS		
Sink(s)	$	$
Faucet(s)	$	$
Countertops	$	$
Shower	$	$
Tub	$	$
Toilet	$	$
Chairs	$	$
Benches/Ottomans	$	$
Side tables	$	$
Shelves/Storage	$	$
Mirrors	$	$

		SHORT TERM	LONG TERM
WINDOW TREATMENTS			
	Hardware	$	$
	Curtains	$	$
	Shades/Blinds	$	$
LIGHTING			
	Wall sconces	$	$
	Picture lights	$	$
	Chandelier	$	$
	Pendant fixtures	$	$
ACCESSORIES			
	Towel rods	$	$
	Linen basket	$	$
	Containers	$	$
	Pictures/Paintings	$	$
	Vases/Ceramics	$	$
	Antiques	$	$
	Plants	$	$
OTHER:			
		$	$
		$	$
		$	$
		$	$
		$	$
		$	$
	TOTAL	$	$

WORKSHEET 1

THE MASTER BATH

$^1/_4{}'' = 1'$

WORKSHEET 2

THE MASTER BATH

$^1/_4" = 1'$

THE BATHROOMS

Maybe you've spared no expense in building the ultimate pampering experience in your master bathroom (see "Space to Indulge—the Master Bath," page 96). What if you've got only one household bathroom—or you have one or two extra ones? As far as your pockets and generosity can stretch, allow all of the bathrooms in your house to express your ability to accommodate your home's other inhabitants or guests. Your design must take into account what type of bathroom it is, who uses it, and what message you want to deliver. For a shared family bathroom, small children, teenagers, or adult family members may be using it routinely. You will want to show your attention to detail in fulfilling their needs for comfort. For a guest bathroom, it will be an opportunity to exhibit your hospitality and creativity. If it's a powder room, you can use a large-scale object or piece of art to bring a sense of importance and drama to such a diminutive room. Despite being the smallest space in your home, a bathroom provides you an opportunity to show off your creative punch. Just because it's a place to clean yourself doesn't mean it has to be sterile in design.

Whether it's for your children or your guests, you should consider their comfort and safety. Consider the texture, hardness, and edges of the surfaces to ensure that no one can get hurt. Fixtures should be intuitively easy to operate and pleasant to the touch. You don't want your guests spending too much time trying to figure out how to get water to flow out of the showerhead or faucet, not to mention feeling a little embarrassed if they need to ask you for instructions. All bathrooms will benefit from bright and ample task lighting allowing users to groom comfortably. Because the light from overhead fixtures often cast harsh shadows on the face, place fixtures on the sides of mirrors when possible.

Exhibit personal touches that go against the preconception that a bathroom is for utilitarian objects only. It can be a spot to exhibit fine art (the kind that can withstand water and steam, of course). You can keep it interesting by suspending a sculptural kinetic mobile over the tub to provide the users with a focal point as they relax. Or you can welcome them into the space with Hollywood glam—a sweeping scarlet velvet shower curtain and sparkling crystal chandelier. Although most people spend little time in the bathroom, do not overlook its potential to comfort and wow them at the same time.

LIFESTYLE QUESTIONNAIRE

What are the primary uses of or the most routine activities in this room?

....

....

....

....

....

What other activities would I like to do in this room?

....

....

....

....

....

What type of environment motivates me to do these activities?

....

....

....

....

....

What do I like most about the room?

....

....

....

What do I like least about the room?

....

....

....

What are my design priorities for this room?

....

....

....

....

....

When does the room receive light?

....

....

....

What mood do I want for this room?

....

....

....

What colors would help me achieve that mood?

....

....

....

What furniture style do I want for this room?

....

....

....

How else can I design this room to achieve the desired mood?

....

....

....

BUDGET SHEET

		SHORT TERM	LONG TERM
FINISHES			
	Wall preparation	$	$
	Paint	$	$
	Wallpaper	$	$
	Tile walls	$	$
	Trim	$	$
FLOORING			
	Carpet	$	$
	Rugs	$	$
	Hardwood	$	$
	Tile/Stone	$	$
	Vinyl/Other	$	$
FIXTURES / FURNISHINGS			
	Sink(s)	$	$
	Faucet(s)	$	$
	Countertops	$	$
	Shower	$	$
	Tub	$	$
	Toilet	$	$
	Chairs	$	$
	Benches/Ottomans	$	$
	Side tables	$	$
	Shelves/Storage	$	$
	Mirrors	$	$

	SHORT TERM	LONG TERM
WINDOW TREATMENTS		
Hardware	$	$
Curtains	$	$
Shades/Blinds	$	$
LIGHTING		
Wall sconces	$	$
Picture lights	$	$
Chandelier	$	$
Pendant fixtures	$	$
ACCESSORIES		
Towel rods	$	$
Linen basket	$	$
Containers	$	$
Pictures/Paintings	$	$
Vases/Ceramics	$	$
Antiques	$	$
Plants	$	$
OTHER:		
	$	$
	$	$
	$	$
	$	$
	$	$
	$	$
TOTAL	$	$

III

WORKSHEET I

THE BATHROOMS

$^1/_4$" = 1'

WORKSHEET 2

THE BATHROOMS

¹/₄" = 1'

APPENDIX

RESOURCES

DESIGN STYLE

If you need some visual stimulation to formulate your personal (or family) design style, you may find these books particularly helpful:

Bilhuber, Jeffrey and Annette Tapert, *Jeffrey Bilhuber's Design Basics: Expert Solutions for Designing the House of Your Dreams.* New York: Rizzoli, 2003.

Evelegh, Tessa, *House Beautiful Decorating School.* New York: Hearst Books, 2004.

Heath, Oliver, *Oliver Heath's Home Book.* London: Cassell Illustrated, 2004.

Hoppen, Kelly, *Kelly Hoppen Style: The Golden Rules of Design.* New York: Bulfinch Press, 2004.

Marshall, Paula (Ed.), *Small House, Big Style.* Des Moines: Better Homes and Garden, 2001.

Trocme, Suzanne, *Attention to Detail: The Finishing Touch in More than 100 Contemporary Rooms.* New York: Stewart, Tabori & Chang, 2004.

Wearstler, Kelly, *Modern Glamour: The Art of Unexpected Style.* New York: Regan Books, 2004.

Wilson, Judith and Debi Treloar, *Family Living: Creating the Perfect Family Home.* New York: Ryland Peters & Small Ltd, 2003.

ROOM SPECIFIC

For books on a particular room in your house:

Copestick, Joanna, *Children's Rooms: Practical Design Solutions for Ages 0-10.* London: Conran Octopus Limited, 2003.

Grey, Johnny, *Kitchen Culture: Reinventing Kitchen Design.* Buffalo: Firefly Books Limited, 2004.

Lee, Vinny, *Kitchens: A Design Sourcebook.* New York: Ryland Peters & Small Ltd, 2002.

Mack, Lorrie, *Calm Working Spaces.* New York: HarperResource, 2000.

Saeks, Diane Dorrans, *Bathrooms (California Design).* San Francisco: Chronicle Books, 1998.

LIGHTING

Whitehead, Randall, *Residential Lighting: A Practical Guide*.
    Hoboken, New Jersey: John Wiley & Sons, Inc., 2003.

Wilhide, Elizabeth, *Lighting: Creative Planning for Successful
    Lighting Solutions*. New York: Ryland Peters & Small
    Ltd, 2004.

COLOR AND TEXTURE

Bowers, Helen, *Interior Materials & Surfaces:
    The Complete Guide*. Buffalo: Firefly Books Ltd, 2005.

Clegg, Emma, *The New Color Book: 45,000 Color Combinations
    for Your Home*. San Francisco: Chronicle Books, 2004.

Guild, Tricia and Elspeth Thompson, *Think Color:
    Rooms to Live In*. San Francisco: Chronicle Books, 2002.

Hanan, Ali, *Color Match for Home Interiors*. Switzerland:
    Rotovision, 2004.

Martin, Cat, *The Surface Texture Bible: More Than 800
    Color and Texture Samples for Every Surfaces, Furnishing,
    and Finish*. New York: Stewart, Tabori & Chang, 2005.

ARRANGING AND DISPLAYING

For books on displaying your treasures:

Butler, David and Amy Butler, *Found Style: Vintage Ideas for
    Modern Living*. San Francisco: Chronicle Books, 2003.

Dilcock, Lesley, *On Display: Displaying Your Treasures With Style*.
    New York: Ryland Peters & Small Ltd, 2002.

Gilchrist, Paige, *At Home With Pictures: Arranging & Displaying
    Photos, Artwork, and Collections*. New York:
    Lark Books, 2004.

HOME ORGANIZATION

Ellis, Casey and Randall Koll, *The Organized Home:
    Design Solutions for Clutter-Free Living*. Gloucester,
    Massachusetts: Lark Books, 2004.

ORGANIZATIONS

If your home redesign project is beyond your technical and physical capabilities, you will likely need to hire some experts to carry
out your vision. These organizations are a good place to start:

American Institute of Architects (AIA)
1735 New York Avenue, NW
Washington, DC 20006
(800) AIA-3837
www.aia.org

American Society of Interior Designers (ASID)
608 Massachusetts Avenue, NE
Washington, DC 20002
(202) 546-3480
www.asid.org

Associated Builders and Contractors
4250 N. Fairfax Drive, 9th Floor
Arlington, VA 22203
(703) 812-2000
www.abc.org

The Associated General Contractors of America
333 John Carlyle Street, Suite 200
Alexandria, VA 22314
(703) 548-3118
www.agc.org

117

CONTACT INFORMATION

STORES/BOUTIQUES

STORE

ADDRESS

PHONE NO.

WEB SITE

STORE

ADDRESS

PHONE NO.

WEB SITE

STORE

ADDRESS

PHONE NO.

WEB SITE

STORE

ADDRESS

PHONE NO.

WEB SITE

ANTIQUE SHOPS

STORE

ADDRESS

PHONE NO.

WEB SITE

STORE

ADDRESS

PHONE NO.

WEB SITE

HARDWARE STORES

STORE

ADDRESS

PHONE NO.

WEB SITE

STORE

ADDRESS

PHONE NO.

WEB SITE

OTHER

STORE ....

ADDRESS ....

....

PHONE NO. ....

WEB SITE ....

STORE ....

ADDRESS ....

....

PHONE NO. ....

WEB SITE ....

STORE ....

ADDRESS ....

....

PHONE NO. ....

WEB SITE ....

STORE ....

ADDRESS ....

....

PHONE NO. ....

WEB SITE ....

WEB SITES

....

....

....

....

....

....

....

....

....

....

....

....

NOTES

121

NOTES

NOTES

125

NOTES

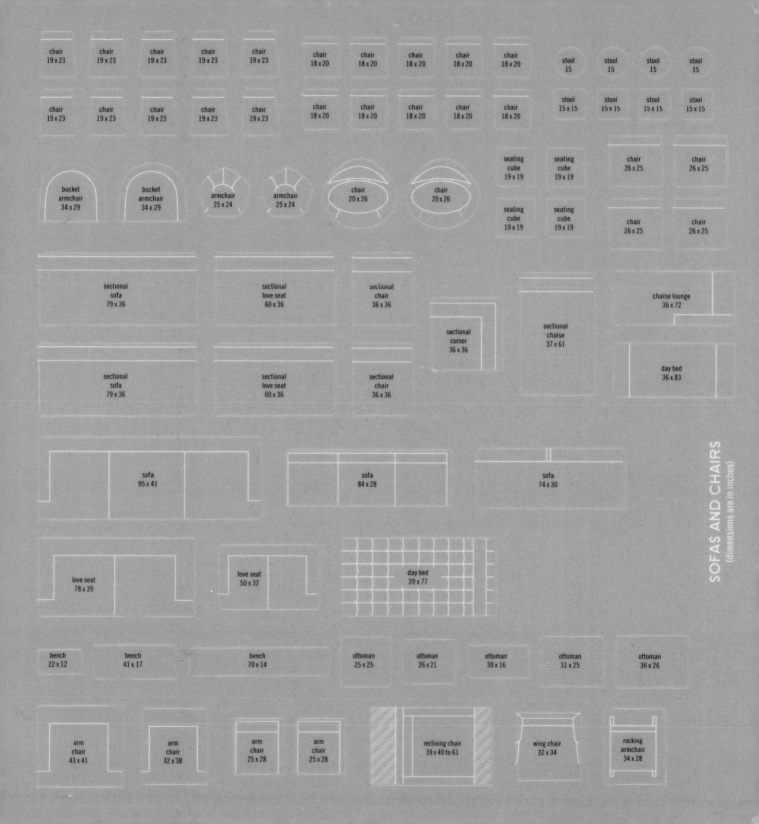

SOFAS AND CHAIRS (dimensions are in inches)

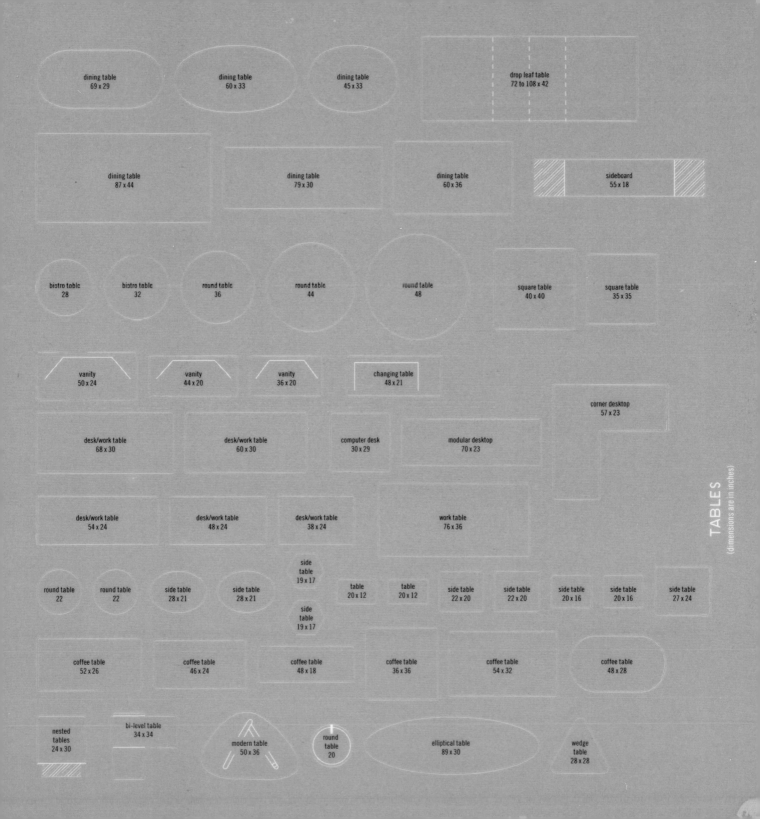

dining table
69 x 29

dining table
60 x 33

dining table
45 x 33

drop leaf table
72 to 108 x 42

dining table
87 x 44

dining table
79 x 30

dining table
60 x 36

sideboard
55 x 18

bistro table
28

bistro table
32

round table
36

round table
44

round table
48

square table
40 x 40

square table
35 x 35

vanity
50 x 24

vanity
44 x 20

vanity
36 x 20

changing table
48 x 21

corner desktop
57 x 23

desk/work table
68 x 30

desk/work table
60 x 30

computer desk
30 x 29

modular desktop
70 x 23

desk/work table
54 x 24

desk/work table
48 x 24

desk/work table
38 x 24

work table
76 x 36

round table
22

round table
22

side table
28 x 21

side table
28 x 21

side
table
19 x 17

table
20 x 12

table
20 x 12

side table
22 x 20

side table
22 x 20

side table
20 x 16

side table
20 x 16

side table
27 x 24

side
table
19 x 17

coffee table
52 x 26

coffee table
46 x 24

coffee table
48 x 18

coffee table
36 x 36

coffee table
54 x 32

coffee table
48 x 28

nested
tables
24 x 30

bi-level table
34 x 34

modern table
50 x 36

round
table
20

elliptical table
89 x 30

wedge
table
28 x 28

TABLES
(dimensions are in inches)

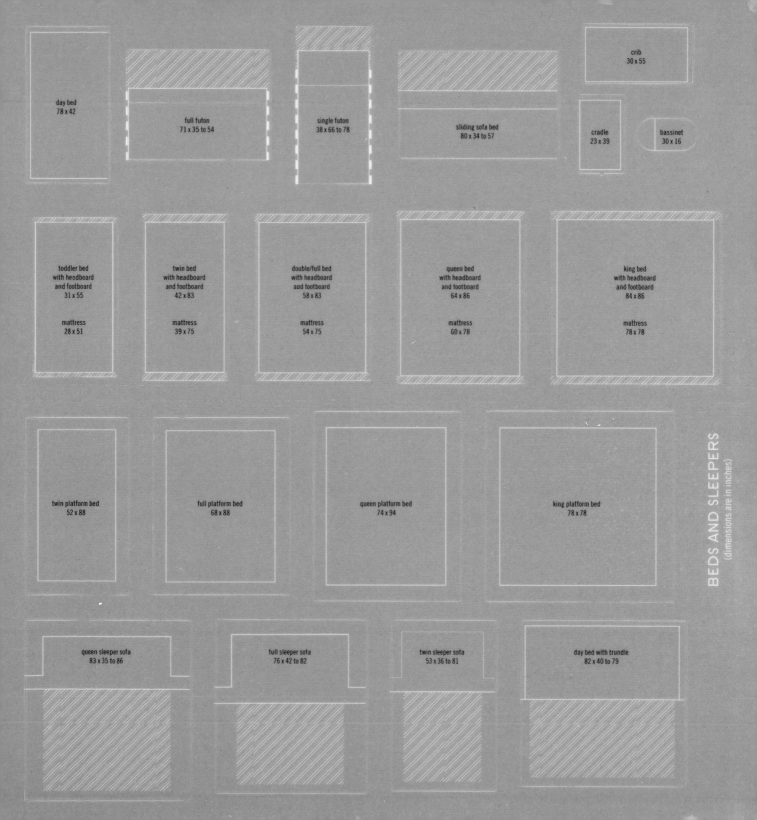

day bed
78 x 42

full futon
71 x 35 to 54

single futon
38 x 66 to 78

sliding sofa bed
80 x 34 to 57

crib
30 x 55

cradle
23 x 39

bassinet
30 x 16

toddler bed
with headboard
and footboard
31 x 55

mattress
28 x 51

twin bed
with headboard
and footboard
42 x 83

mattress
39 x 75

double/full bed
with headboard
and footboard
58 x 83

mattress
54 x 75

queen bed
with headboard
and footboard
64 x 86

mattress
60 x 78

king bed
with headboard
and footboard
84 x 86

mattress
78 x 78

twin platform bed
52 x 88

full platform bed
68 x 88

queen platform bed
74 x 94

king platform bed
78 x 78

queen sleeper sofa
83 x 35 to 86

full sleeper sofa
76 x 42 to 82

twin sleeper sofa
53 x 36 to 81

day bed with trundle
82 x 40 to 79

BEDS AND SLEEPERS
(dimensions are in inches)

television stand
58 x 24

television stand
62 x 23

television stand
44 x 25

television stand
41 x 22

widescreen tv
48 x 22

widescreen tv
53 x 25

media cabinet
98 x 26

media cabinet
71 x 28

media cabinet
34 x 18

piano
56 x 24

console
54 x 16

console
48 x 14

console
32 x 13

console
48 x 15

piano
40 x 24

grand piano
59 x 56

credenza
81 x 19

credenza
63 x 28

corner cabinet
34 x 34

corner cabinet
34 x 34

cabinet
24 x 17

cabinet
14 x 11

cabinet
18 x 15

cart
23 x 18

cart
39 x 16

cart
24 x 24

etagere
15 x 15

etagere
19 x 19

cabinet
53 x 18

cabinet
41 x 19

cabinet
24 x 17

cabinet
14 x 11

cabinet
18 x 15

file cabinet
21 x 17

shelves
30 x 12

shelves
30 x 12

corner
24 x 12

leaning shelf
32 x 16

leaning shelf
32 x 16

leaning shelf
32 x 16

lateral file cabinet
35 x 21

lateral file cabinet
41 x 17

file cabinet
21 x 17

shelves
30 x 12

shelves
30 x 12

corner
24 x 12

bookcase
34 x 11

bookcase
34 x 11

bookcase
94 x 12

bookcase
71 x 14

bookcase
58 x 14

bookcase
45 x 15

bookcase
36 x 16

bookcase
94 x 12

bookcase
71 x 14

bookcase
58 x 14

bookcase
45 x 15

bookcase
36 x 16

armoire
54 x 29

armoire
40 x 28

armoire
33 x 24

storage trunk
45 x 20

storage trunk
41 x 17

dresser
24 x 19

dresser
24 x 19

dresser
32 x 18

dresser
65 x 22

dresser
66 x 20

dresser
33 x 22

dresser
48 x 22

wine bar
18 x 13

wine rack
20 x 15

hutch cabinet
45 x 20

wine bar
18 x 13

bar
38 x 18

buffet
67 x 17

buffet
66 x 22

buffet
42 x 19

wine rack
20 x 15

wine bar
18 x 13

hutch cabinet
53 x 21

MEDIA / ORGANIZATION
(dimensions are in inches)

base cabinet
39 x 24

base cabinet
39 x 24

base cabinet
39 x 24

base cabinet
39 x 24

base cabinet
18 x 24

base cabinet
18 x 24

base cabinet
18 x 24

base cabinet
18 x 24

base cabinet
36 x 24

base cabinet
36 x 24

base cabinet
36 x 24

base cabinet
36 x 24

base cabinet
15 x 24

base cabinet
15 x 24

base cabinet
15 x 24

base cabinet
15 x 24

base cabinet
24 x 24

base cabinet
24 x 24

base cabinet
24 x 24

base cabinet
24 x 24

base cabinet
12 x 24

base cabinet
12 x 24

base cabinet
12 x 24

base cabinet
12 x 24

base cabinet
36 x 36

dishwasher
24 x 26

refrigerator
28 x 28

refrigerator
29 x 36

refrigerator
35 x 30

refrigerator
36 x 32

refrigerator
48 x 32

sink unit
24 x 21

sink unit
36 x 21

sink unit
36 x 21

range
20 x 25

range
24 x 26

range
30 x 26

range
36 x 26

range
40 x 25

range
48 x 27

corner cabinet
36 x 34

corner cabinet
42 x 42

single vanity
39 x 22

single vanity
24 x 23

single vanity
42 x 24

double vanity
49 x 22

double washstand
31 x 18

rectangular basin
24 x 21

kitchen island
48 x 24

single vanity
39 x 22

single vanity
24 x 23

single vanity
42 x 24

double vanity
52 x 24

double washstand
47 x 22

rectangular basin
24 x 21

kitchen island
57 x 25

basin
14

basin
14

pedestal basin
22 x 18

pedestal basin
22 x 18

toilet
20 x 27

toilet
18 x 26

toilet
15 x 24

toilet
14 x 20

bidet
14 x 22

bidet
14 x 22

square shower
35 x 35

rectangle shower
47 x 29

rectangle shower
39 x 27

square shower
27 x 27

pentangle shower
43 x 35

corner bathtub
55 x 55

round bathtub/spa
35

round bathtub/spa
43

round bathtub/spa
55

traditional roll-top bathtub
69 x 31

rectangle bathtub
67 x 27

CABINETS / APPLIANCES
(dimensions are in inches)